Old Pollokshields
Sandra Malcolm

In 1871 Glasgow Corporation obtained powers to lay down tramlines for horsedrawn trams. The Glasgow Transport and Omnibus Company leased the system for 23 years until 1894. At the end of the lease the company and Glasgow Corporation could not come to any agreement, so the corporation took over the lines under special powers of the 1870 Corporation Act. On 1 July 1894 the corporation began its new service and over the years, thanks to a strong desire to expand the services throughout the city, the lines ran into numerous suburbs and adjacent towns. In 1899 the decision was taken to prepare for the electrification of the tramlines and land was purchased to build the main generating station - Pinkston Power Station - on the north bank of the Forth and Clyde Canal. There were five sub-stations situated round the city – Partick, Dalhousie, Kinning Park, Whitevale and Coplawhill – and nine car sheds, at Partick, Possilpark, Maryhill, Dennistoun, Whitevale, Dalmarnock, Pollokshaws, Langside and Kinning Park. In this photograph the car being worked on at Coplawhill is number 797 which was constructed around 1900 and scrapped in 1959.

Dating from 1878, Pollokshields Church of Scotland was designed by Robert Baldie and built at a cost of £14,000. It replaced the adjoining church hall at 525 Shields Road, seen here behind the church. The interior of the church has a wealth of stained glass, many panels of which are dedicated in memory of local businessmen. Most of the glass was designed by Stephen Adam. Although Baldie's main business was in church work, he also designed a scheme for sewage treatment in Glasgow. Alterations were made to the church by H.E. Clifford. These included changes to the vestry, vestibule and session room. He also designed the oak cases for the organ. The original 1878 organ was replaced by a new one in 1913, built by Arthur Harrison and Alfred Heap, and the opening recital was given by Sir Frederick Bridge of Westminster Abbey.

© Sandra Malcolm, 2010
First published in the United Kingdom, 2010,
by Stenlake Publishing Ltd.
www.stenlake.co.uk
ISBN 9781840335248

The publishers regret that they cannot supply copies of any pictures featured in this book.

Acknowledgements

Many thanks to those who patiently put up with my researches and to mum and dad for helping show me the value of history. The photographs on page 42 were taken by A.D. Packer and appear here with his permission.

Further Reading

The books and websites listed below were used by the author during her research. None of the books is available from Stenlake Publishing. Those interested in finding out more are advised to contact their local bookshop or reference library.

www.theglasgowstory.com
www.scran.ac.uk
www.friendsofmaxwellpark.co.uk
www.pollokshieldsheritage.org
www.titwoodlawntennisclub.co.uk
www.titwoodbowlingclub.co.uk
www.pollokshieldsburghhall.com

Joseph D. Hendry, *A Social History of Branch Library Development*, Scottish Library Association 1974.
Andrew Jeffrey, *This Time of Crisis*, Mainstream Publishing 1993.
Duncan McLellan, *Glasgow Public Parks*, John Smith & Son 1894.
John Guthrie Smith and John Oswald Mitchell, *The Old Country Houses of the Old Glasgow Gentry*, 1878.
Ronald Smith, *Pollokshields Historical Guide and Heritage Walk*, 1998.
Ian G. McM. Stewart, *The Glasgow Tramcar*, Scottish Tramway Museum Society 1994.
Williamson, Riches, Higgs, *The Buildings of Scotland – Glasgow*, Penguin 1990.
Frank Wordsall, *The Glasgow Tenement*, Chambers 1979.
Frank Wordsall, *The City That Disappeared*, Richard Drew Publishing 1981.
Frank Wordsall, *Victorian City*, Richard Drew Publishing 1982.

Introduction

The lands of Pollok formed part of the extensive estates which were granted by King David I to Walter the High Steward about the year 1124. The grant of David was confirmed by his grandson, King Malcolm IV, in 1157/58. Part of the lands of Pollok was bestowed by the High Steward on Peter, son of Fulbert, who was one of his followers, and whose immediate descendants adopted the territorial designation of Pollok. They were vassals of the Steward, who continued to be the Superior of Upper Pollok. This superiority was acquired by Rolland de Mearns to whom the ancient family of Maxwell of Nether Pollok can trace its origins back to the thirteenth century when Roland de Mearns' heir, Mary, married Sir Aymer Maxwell of Caerlaverock. The ancient barony of Mearns and Pollok thus came into the hands of the Maxwells. In 1270, Sir Aymer Maxwell granted to his third son, Sir John Maxwell, the lower division of the barony, or Nether Pollok.

The first castle of the Maxwells, probably built by Sir John, was close to the River Cart, but no traces of it remain today. The second castle which was inhabited until the middle of the sixteenth century was built close by and a third castle was built about 1367, on the site of the first. Known as the 'laighe place', it was the residence of the dowagers and young lairds, whilst the knight or baronet in possession occupied the other, principal castle. Haggs Castle, which was built about 1585, afterwards became the dowager house, and the 'Laighe Castle' was then the chief residence of the family.

In 1676, Sir George Maxwell took part in a witch trial in Gourock. Shortly afterwards he believed himself bewitched, suffering a 'hot and fiery distemper'. A local deaf and dumb girl, Janet Douglas, who had been seen around the servants' quarters, disclosed that his effigies were to be found stuck with pins at the house of Janet Mathie, widow to the miller of Shaw Mill. Janet, her son John Stewart (supposedly a warlock), her daughter Annabel and another three women were tried in Paisley in 1677. Annabel was only 14 years old, and was released, but the others were burned at the stake. Sir George recovered but lived for only a few months. After the trial Janet Douglas appeared to recover her speech and hearing, but suspicion fell on her because she continued her self-appointed witch hunt. The Privy Council decided she should be banished from Scotland, but no captain of any ship would take her on board, so she was allowed to disappear.

In 1747 Sir John Maxwell, 3rd Baronet, pulled the 'Laighe Castle' down, and built the present mansion house. It was finished in 1752, and some small additions were made in 1845/46.

In 1790 Pollok was still very rural, with a population of around 3,000. Less than 100 years later, the population stood at around 100,000. Sir John Maxwell, 8th Baronet, had the idea of laying out a garden suburb and in 1849 he commissioned David Rhind (the architect responsible for the Scott Monument in Edinburgh) to draw up plans for the open fields to the south of the Glasgow, Paisley & Ardrossan Canal. Very little of Rhind's plans came to fruition, but the distinct characteristics of West Pollokshields and East Pollokshields stem from that time. The western end mainly developed through villa building and the eastern end was predominantly tenemental. The Maxwells laid down strict feuing conditions and in West Pollokshields shops and trades were forbidden and no two villas were allowed to be of the same design.

The Burgh of Pollokshields was formed in 1876 and only included the western area with a population of 1,518. In 1880 the Burgh of East Pollokshields was formed with a population of 4,360. By the time Glasgow expanded its boundaries in 1891 to include Pollokshields, the population of East Pollokshields was 6,681 and West Pollokshields 3,798. Building continued in the area until the inter-war period and by the 1950s many of the properties suffered from neglect. Many of the large villas were turned into flats or converted into institutions. In the 1950s Glasgow Corporation bought many villas to use the land for high-density council housing. Many of these were in St Andrew's Drive and the north side of Maxwell Drive. Local people became concerned with the destruction of Pollokshields and formed the Pollokshields Preservation and Development Association. The corporation decided to preserve the area after pressure from the association and designated it a Conservation Area in 1973, protecting the trees as well as the buildings.

Photographed outside the Albert Drive entrance to the Coplawhill Tramcar Works, the Pickfords truck is carrying one of Liverpool Council's 'Green Goddess' trams bought by Glasgow Corporation in 1953 to augment its fleet. It is believed that the Pickford family, originally from Adlington, near Manchester, first entered the business of moving goods around in the seventeenth century. By 1646 the Pickfords owned a quarry and in order to make best use of their wagons, they carried goods for others when their own wagons were empty. Business must have been successful as by 1720 James Pickford had his headquarters in London. In 1771 the Pickfords inverted the fly wagon, which could cover the journey from London to Manchester in four and a half days. By 1779 the company owned 50 wagons and 400 horses. In 1814 after a number of years of decline the company almost became bankrupt, but the family saved the company by selling to new owners, Joseph Baxendale, Charles Inman and Zachary Langton. The Baxendale family remained active in the company until 1932. It was Joseph Baxendale who realised the potential of the railways and made sure that he joined the boards of several railway companies in order to increase Pickfords' business. Between 1918 and 1921, the company had 1,580 horses, 1,900 horse vehicles and 46 motor vehicles. In 1919 its main business was in removals and it was sold to the Hayes Wharf Company Ltd. In 1921 the Saurer Motor Company in Switzerland started to manufacture high quality heavy petrol wagons and this began the end of their reliance on steam traction for heavy loads. In 1946 the company was nationalised to form part of British Road Services and in 1963 Pickfords became part of the National Freight Corporation owned by the Treasury. However, in 1969 there was an employee buyout and in 1982 it was introduced to the stock exchange. Pickfords became part of SIRVA in 1995 and in 2002 Kevin Pickford became managing director of Pickford UK. By 2009 Pickfords had moved its headquarters to Wembley after being sold by SIRVA to a private owner.

This 1959 photograph of Coronation tram number 1232 was taken in Albert Drive. The tram came into service on 12 December 1938 and was withdrawn on 1 September 1962. Coronation trams were the 'new luxury trams' that were built to replace the ageing Standards. In 1938 Glasgow hosted the Empire Exhibition at Bellahouston Park; meanwhile, Glasgow Corporation ordered a fleet of 100 trams to be built, the first of which was delivered in 1937. The Transport Department named the new trams 'Exhibition Trams', but the popular name given to them by the public was 'Coronation', 1937 being the year of King George VI's coronation. A total of 150 cars were built and were described as the finest short stage carriage vehicles in Europe.

Coplawhill Tramcar Works began in 1893 as a horse-tram depot built for the takeover by Glasgow Corporation of horse-tram services in the city. From 1820 to 1862 this site had been partially occupied by the 40-acre market garden called Coplaw Nursery. When the city tramways were electrified in 1899/1900, tramcar building and maintenance workshops were added. The paint shop, shown here, was a large department employing 49 men and the paint was made up on the premises. The shop could accommodate 30 trams at a time. The lettering of the trams was done in aluminium transfers as silver paint could not withstand the high levels of sulphur in Glasgow's atmosphere. Glasgow trams had special seats, known as the 'Glasgow seat', which was invented by a rolling-stock superintendent, Mr Ferguson. The seat was designed so that rainwater could run through the grooves and drop through drilled holes, thus ensuring it would easily dry off.

This photograph shows the tinsmith's shop at the Coplawhill works. There was also a brass foundry where all brass fittings were cast. The smithy, as the tinsmith's shop was known, covered 800 square yards and manufactured metalwork for the trams. During the First World War James Dalrymple, General Manager of the Corporation Tramways, encouraged the war effort by using Coplawhill as a recruiting hall. It took 16 hours to enlist 1,012 men to the 15th Battalion HLI (which was entirely made up from men from the Transport Department). A few of the tramway engineering sections at the depot were converted to making munitions, and the factory also produced wings for FE 2B planes and BE 2C aircraft.

Over 3,000 men left the Transport Department to join the forces during the First World War and one in six of these men never returned. Because of the shortage of men, the department was the first of any city to introduce women conductresses and drivers. In 1918, the department employed 1,292 men and 266 women.

To the right of the paint shop was the tram body shop, where the finishing work and joinery were executed. Coplawhill also boasted its own large sawmill, almost the same size as the smithy, which dealt with coachwork and interior furnishings. The sawmill was heated by overhead pipes and the air was kept clean by automatic suction fans which sent all the debris straight to the furnace. The Transport Department was keen to provide clubs for its employees, and workers could join any number of groups for sports such as football, swimming, golf, bowls and billiards. In addition there were ambulance classes and radio classes. The Departmental Choir held annual concerts in St Andrews Halls and the orchestra was often engaged to play in Glasgow's parks. The pipe band won the World Championship Trophy on more than one occasion.

To become a driver (or motorman), an employee had to have at least one year's experience as a conductor. The department had to be sure that their drivers would uphold the motto of 'Safety, Courtesy and Efficiency'. The course to be a motorman lasted 12 days and took place at Coplawhill where the department had a tram in skeleton form with an inspection pit underneath to help train their men. After four days of training, trainees would have four days of practice on a service tram. Then they had to return to the school for an examination and, if they passed that, they would receive more training until their final examination on Day 12. If they passed, they then had 30 days of probation before becoming fully qualified motormen. Each member of traffic staff had a summer and winter uniform and it was expected that all employees would be smartly dressed at all times. The lost property office at Coplawhill had a category of 'miscellaneous' to cover such items as false teeth, wooden legs, caged birds and even tombstones. In 1931, 55,984 items were handed in as lost property. After the demise of the trams in the 1960s, Coplawhill was no longer required and the building came into use as Glasgow's Museum of Transport. In 1986 the museum moved to Kelvin Hall and the building was left vacant, with the threat of demolition hanging over it. However, it was turned into a performance arts venue in time for Glasgow's reign as European City of Culture in 1990 and the Tramway became internationally renowned after the only UK performances of Peter Brook's *Mahabharata*. In 2003 the Hidden Gardens were opened, appropriately, on the site of the nineteenth-century Coplawhill Nursery just behind the venue. Recently, the Tramway also became home to the new headquarters for Scottish Ballet.

The Burgh Hall was built at the northeastern end of Maxwell Park. Opened in 1890, it was designed by H.E. Clifford, the Burgh Architect, in the Scots Renaissance style of the seventeenth century. Just after its completion, the burgh became part of Glasgow. The red sandstone came from Ballochmyle in Ayrshire and many of the stained glass windows were gifts from local residents. The Burgh Sanitary Inspector and the Park Keeper were the first occupants of the two flats in the lodge house built at the side. The Maxwell family coat of arms is carved above the entrance porch of the hall, flanked by two Scottish lions, and is also recorded in marble in the vestibule floor. The 60-foot high tower, housing a turret stair, corbelled balcony and vigil windows, dominates the exterior of the building. It was also used as a Masonic meeting place, hence the numerous Masonic symbols in the carvings and in the stained glass windows. The first lodge to meet there was Lodge Pollok, Pollokshields No. 772 on 25 October 1890. On that occasion the Foundation Stone was laid in the vestibule by Brother Sir John Stirling Maxwell of Pollok. In 1991 the hall was taken over by a charitable trust who acquired it for £1 and much restoration work was carried out. A large portion of the funds for this came from Heritage Lottery Funding.

Maxwell Park was presented to the burgh by Sir John Stirling Maxwell in 1878. He wished to provide a place of recreation and amusement for his feuars. The Commissioners of Pollokshields enclosed the land with a railing and carried out extensive drainage works as the land was known to be mossy. When digging out the drains many stems and roots were found, principally of oak trees. This led to the belief that the area must have been covered by a large forest at one time. On 13 August 1893 a census of visitors to the park was taken between 6 a.m. and 10 p.m. A staggering 9,500 people entered the park that day.

Maxwell Park only covers 21 acres of land and is the smallest in Glasgow. Glasgow Corporation laid off a plot near the main entrance as an American flower garden, planted principally with rhododendrons, azaleas, kalmias, menezias and acubas. It was hoped that when all the plants were well established there would be little need for maintenance.

The park's fountain was designed in 1907 by Burnet, Boston and Carruthers in French Renaissance style and was made of Carrara stoneware by Doulton & Co. The unveiling ceremony on 11 March 1908 was performed by Lady McOnie and the water was turned on by Lady Ure Primrose. The statue at the top of the 10.75-metre column was of Thomas Hamilton, a local baker, victualler and grain merchant who used to hunt in the area before the park was formed. The portrait medallion was of his son John. The fountain was the gift of Elizabeth Millar Hamilton and her sister Christina Brown Primrose Hamilton to commemorate their father and brother. They wanted the fountain to be exactly in the centre of the park but by that time the bandstand was already there and it was too costly to resite it. Over the years the fountain fell into disrepair and was finally demolished in 1989 because there was no funding for repair or maintenance. The only evidence that remains is the large flowerbed created with the edging of the original basin.

The commissioners also formed roads and walks within the park and trees and shrubs were planted along them. When Pollokshields East and West became part of Glasgow in 1891, alterations and improvements were made to the park by the corporation. A bandstand was erected as well as drinking fountains, waiting rooms, a putting green and a tennis court. All these have disappeared over the years as a result of neglect, lack of funding, lack of use or vandalism.

When Glasgow Corporation took over the park a number of byelaws were passed. There were laws against beating or shaking carpets; singing, preaching or lecturing; being intoxicated or using profane language; discharging fire arms or fireworks; taking part in a picnic or luncheon party; making a bonfire; allowing any horse, pony, donkey, cow, goat, sheep or pig to enter the park; and there were to be no bicycles, velocipedes, wheelbarrows, carts and carriages. Any person caught contravening any of the byelaws would be liable to a fine not exceeding £5.

When the park was laid out, it was already known that the land was waterlogged and mossy, and so it had to be drained. The surface water was drained to the lowest point of the park, new drainage was put in and the pond was formed. This was used for model yachts in the summer. In 1892 the Maxwell Model Yacht Club complained about the pollution of the pond by oil from the Glasgow South Model Yacht Club's yachts. In winter, the frozen pond was used for skating and in 1895 2,000 skaters were counted using it in one day. The Model Steamer Club, now based in Thornliebank, was originally based in Maxwell Park.

Pollokshields District Library was one of 12 Glasgow libraries to receive funding from Andrew Carnegie. It cost around £5,000 and was designed by Thomas Gilmour of Glasgow's City Engineer's Department. Gilmour's competition-winning design was revised by his superior, Alexander B. McDonald. It has exterior panels inscribed 'Literature', 'History', 'The Arts' and inside the building there is stained glass designed and made by John Hall. It was officially opened on 20 February 1907 by Sir John Stirling Maxwell who paid 'a tribute of gratitude to Andrew Carnegie for all he has done on behalf of public libraries in the United Kingdom'. In 1932 the Libraries Committee had to make cuts to reduce their expenditure and Pollokshields Library was one of five to be temporarily closed. After receiving numerous complaints about this, the libraries were reopened the following year.

Sir John Ure Primrose was senior partner of the firm of Messrs William Primrose & Sons, Centre Street Flour Mills, Glasgow. Born on 6 October 1847 he first got involved in public life as a member of Govan Police Commission. He first represented the Kingston Ward in Glasgow in 1886, and continued to be re-elected. From 1891 to 1895, he was a magistrate and became Glasgow's Master of Works in 1902, succeeding Sir Samuel Chisholm as Lord Provost in 1903. It was he who secured the erection of the fire station in Ingram Street and he was created a baronet in May 1903. The opening of Hampden Football ground was performed by him in 1903, although he was more closely allied with Rangers Football Club than Queen's Park. On Saturday 2 January 1909 the *Scotsman* reported that there had been an unfortunate incident involving Sir John at the football match between Rangers and Celtic. 'A collection was being made during the course of the game on behalf of the Eastpark Home for Children, when a man to whom the box was offered seized it for some reason and threw it away. The box fell among the spectators in the stand and struck the hat of a gentleman, smashing it completely. Rebounding, the box hit Sir John Ure Primrose Bart. behind the ear and inflicted a nasty cut. Sir John was medically attended, but fortunately the injury proved comparatively slight …. The individual who threw the box was arrested by the police, but Sir John interceded for him, and it is unlikely that further proceedings will be taken.' Sir John's residence, seen here, was at 'Redholme', 271 Nithsdale Road at Dalgarvel Avenue. The ground is now occupied by a block of modern flats. He also owned Cairndhu House in Helensburgh, designed by William Leiper.

Haggs Castle in St Andrew's Drive was built by Sir John Maxwell (1585–1587) and was used as a jointure house (i.e. it was granted to a wife for the period in which she survived after the death of her husband). During the mid to late 1600s the castle was associated with the struggles of the Covenanters. Sir John Maxwell was fined £8,000 for allowing them on his land and he was imprisoned in 1676 for holding banned religious services inside the castle. After 1752 it became derelict when Sir John Maxwell, 3rd Baronet (d. 1752), completed the building of a new residence, Pollok House. By 1840 the lower floor was occupied by a smithy associated with the local coal mine. The castle was restored around 1860 by Sir John Maxwell, 9th Baronet, and was occupied by the Pollok Estate's factor, Mr Colledge (d. 1899). During the Second World War the government used it for military purposes and after the war it was divided into four residences. Glasgow Corporation bought the property and from 1972 it housed Glasgow's Museum of Childhood. In 1998 it reverted to residential use as a house with 19 bedrooms.

Maxwell Park Station, built by the Caledonian Railway Company, opened in 1894 when the Cathcart Railway (which had opened in 1886) was extended to become the Cathcart Circle. It was designed by Frank Colledge along with the other Cathcart Circle stations. All the Circle stations had distinctive island platforms and the trains ran every ten minutes between 8 a.m. and 8 p.m. The wagons bringing masonry blocks for new villas and tenements were delivered to the nearby goods line when it first opened. Although first suggested in 1899, electrification of the Circle was completed in 1962. The station was de-staffed in 1986. Railtrack carried out a reconstruction of the exterior station hall in 1999/2000 but the internal shell remained unoccupied. Towards the end of 2008 Pollokshields Heritage entered into an arrangement with First Scotrail under their Adopt-a-Station scheme and have received grants from Glasgow City Council's South Area committee and the Railway Heritage Trust to refurbish the former ticket office at street level into a meeting room available for small community group meetings.

The church in the centre of this photograph of Maxwell Square was Pollokshields United Presbyterian Church, which began as a hall church in Herriet Street in 1879. The architect of the hall was W.F. McGibbon and it was his first attempt at an ecclesiastical design. He was so successful that he was allowed to design the church seen here, which opened between 1882/83. The site was a sloping one, so he designed the basement area for extra rooms and halls. The frontage was on the lowest part of the site with the church on a raised level. He used flying buttresses to link the nave and side aisles. Inside, the galleries were fitted into the side aisles and separated from the nave by four arches. Extra light came into the building from a clerestory and at the north end an arch opened into the organ chamber. Some patterned glass was put in the windows, although over the years many stained glass windows were gifted by members of the congregation. The church was destroyed by fire in 1983.

The corner of Kenmure Street and Melville Street, *c.*1908. Just beside Maxwell Square, in Melville Street, is the oldest purpose-built school in Pollokshields. It was opened in 1879 as Pollokshields Public School under the auspices of Govan Parish School Board. Designed by H. & D. Barclay, it had an associated janitor's house beside it. On 21 March 1882 a playground shelter collapsed on top of 30 children. Two girls were found dead and another boy and girl died shortly afterwards from their injuries. In May of that same year, David Barclay, the architect, and four workers were charged with culpable homicide. At the trial, they were found not guilty on the criminal charge, but Govan Parish School Board was found to be negligent through lack of proper supervision. In 1926 the school became Pollokshields Primary School and was until recently used as the Infant Department. In 2009, following an amalgamation in the summer, the whole school is now altogether in Albert Drive. The Melville Street building is to be refurbished as an Early Years centre.

Maxwell Square was originally intended as the centrepiece of East Pollokshields. It opened in 1889 and covered three quarters of an acre. Sir John Stirling Maxwell gifted the land as a park to provide green space for local children. The ground level of the square was nine feet below that of the surrounding streets, so to compensate for this, the surface was raised by six feet and covered with ashes and fresh turf. It boasted a cast-iron drinking fountain and seats and was considered to be a model children's playground. However, by 1891, there were numerous complaints from residents about the disorderly behaviour that took place there in the evenings. During the Second World War a large air raid precaution water tank was sited in the square along with a mooring block for a barrage balloon.

The typical three-storey tenements of Pollokshields are seen here on the left of this view of Glencairn Drive. The block shown dates from 1883 and was named after Olrig in Caithness. The tenements have bowed and turreted bays, with many classical details over the windows and doors. The 170-feet high church tower seen on the right was originally part of Pollokshields Free Church. The tower is modelled on St George's Tron in the centre of Glasgow. Built in 1875/76, the church seated 1,020 to the design of McKissack & Rowan. Later it became Pollokshields West Church of Scotland, and then the Nithsdale Trust Church of the Plymouth Brethren. It is now used as a nursing home.

Glencairn Drive (branching off to the left) and Nithsdale Road, May 1928. The architect of many of the buildings and houses in Pollokshields was Henry Edward Clifford, born at North Naparama, Trinidad, in 1852. In 1859 Clifford's father died of a stroke and his mother brought the family to Glasgow. In October 1867 Clifford was articled to John Burnet Senior for five years and after 10 years learning his trade, he left to set up his own practice, having won £100 in a newspaper competition to design a workman's cottage. By 1884 his practice began to thrive, and he took rooms at 140 Bath Street, within the office of the architect John Honeyman. In 1885 he formed a partnership with Burnet's nephew and former assistant William Landless as Landless & Clifford at 227 West George Street. The partnership broke up in 1887 and Clifford practised on his own from several addresses in St Vincent Street, much of the business being around Campbeltown. His home address between 1877 and throughout the 1880s was his mother and sisters' school in Pollokshields, first at 13 (now 167) Nithsdale Road and later in Moray Place. In the early 1890s he built himself a weekend house at Troon, but continued to live in Pollokshields during the week. In 1905 he married and in 1911, two years after his son was born, he built a new house in Elphinstone Road, Whitecraigs. It was named Woodbrook after the Trinidad estate. In 1901 he won the Glasgow Royal Infirmary competition but following a difference of opinion between the directors and their assessor, Rowand Anderson, the commission was given to James Miller. On 11 June 1906 Clifford was elected FRIBA. After going into partnership with Thomas Lunan, they won the competition assessed by Burnet for the new City Hall at Perth. However, Lunan's health was seriously affected by his war experiences and Clifford bought out his partnership. Clifford continued on his own until his retirement in 1923. His practice was absorbed by that of Watson & Salmond.

On the left hand side of this view of Albert Road is St Albert's Roman Catholic Church. In 1886 the building opened as a United Free Presbyterian church, having been designed by J.B. Wilson and built at a cost of £8,845. Between 1887 and 1909 it was known as the Stockwell Free Church, and then as Albert Drive United Free Church of Scotland. The congregation joined the Church of Scotland in 1929. In 1965 the church was sold to the Roman Catholic Church and a two-storey presbytery was erected diagonally opposite. Just beside the church is Glenapp Street (originally Cadder Street), across from which are New Victoria Gardens where 60 allotments were established in 1877, having started in Govanhill in 1865 as Victoria Gardens. Facilities include storage, running water and standpipes and toilets. Every year there is an annual show, a tradition that started in 1887. Named after Queen Victoria's husband, the present Albert Drive runs from Pollokshaws Road to St Andrew's Drive. From 1870 the part from Shields Road to Nithsdale Road was known as Albert Road and from Shields Road to Pollokshaws Road was Albert Street. In 1882 the former was changed to Albert Drive and the latter to Albert Road.

The area where Kenmure Street crosses Albert Drive was known as Albert Cross. It was designed to be the commercial centre of the Burgh of East Pollokshields and the corner details of the tenements (which were not allowed to be higher than three storeys in Pollokshields) such as mansard roofs and gabled dormers reflected its importance. Off to the left is Leslie Street where the Home Guard had a battalion stationed during the Second World War. Glasgow had 23,000 men in 12 city battalions, and Pollokshields' was the 12th (Works South East) Battalion boasting almost 3,200 men. On the night of Monday, 7 April 1941, bombs fell opposite the junction of Kenmure Street and St Andrew's Road and many houses were damaged. Around 120 people were rendered homeless and were sent to the rest centre at Pollokshields Primary School. When they got there, the janitor refused them entry on the grounds that he hadn't had instructions from the Welfare Department!

Car 1089 (known as 'Bailie Burt's Car' possibly after the convenor of the Corporation Tramways Committee) and Car 1269 are seen here in Albert Drive in 1962. The single-decker tram was originally built in 1926 as an experimental high-speed vehicle with a separate entrance and exit. To begin with it was operated from Langside on the Sinclair Drive service and was used to train motormen on air brakes before the Standard cars were fitted with this modification. The cross seats were reportedly very comfortable 'for those fortunate enough to get on them' and the lack of seats forced too many passengers to stand. This also made it difficult to collect fares. In 1932 it was converted to normal use. It was used on a number of different routes until mid-June 1961. It was painted for the closing procession on 4 September 1962 and thereafter was on display in the Museum of Transport. Car 1269 began service in 1939 and was withdrawn in June 1962.

Albert Road Academy, in the foreground of this photograph, opened in 1879 at 241 Albert Road. Designed by Hugh and David Barclay, it was commissioned by Govan Parish School Board. There was insufficient space in the building for the numbers of pupils and in 1882 a sister school opened nearby as Albert Road Public School (this is the building in the background of the photograph). In 1926 the schools combined as Albert Road Academy, with Pollokshields Public School on Melville Street becoming its Primary Department. The academy was later renamed Pollokshields Senior Secondary School and when secondary pupils were moved to Bellahouston Academy in 1962, the original two school buildings became Pollokshields Primary School. Hannah Frank (1908–2008), the Glasgow artist and sculptor, was a pupil at Albert Road Academy before going to the University of Glasgow. She graduated in 1930, having had many poems and drawings published by Glasgow University Magazine under the pseudonym Al Aaraaf. After university she trained as a teacher at Jordanhill College of Education and followed a career in teaching while attending Glasgow School of Art in the evenings. In the 1950s she took up sculpture, having being encouraged by Benno Schotz. Much of her work has been on exhibition throughout the country.

Another view of Albert Road Academy. In September 1894, Mrs Jessie Murdoch opened Pollokshields Ladies School at 63 Dalziel Drive, a house called Craigholme. There were 40 pupils on the roll. By 1918 the school had adopted the name Craigholme and took boys up to the age of nine and girls up to the age of 14. By 1937 the roll had increased and the senior pupils moved to premises at 72 St Andrew's Drive. The school was evacuated to the Trossachs at the start of the Second World War and in 1940, when the school returned, both junior and senior pupils were based in St Andrew's Drive because the roll had fallen. In 1942 the school was sold to the Pollok School Company, a group of parents and businessmen who bought the school to allow it to continue. Despite the fall in numbers, more premises were purchased at 328 Albert Drive, an investment that paid off when, as expansion continued in 1955, more property was bought at 68 St Andrew's Drive. In 1959, with money from Glaxo, a basement corridor was built to link all three houses. In 1963 houses in Hamilton Drive were purchased, but 328 Albert Drive would not sell. As a result, the kindergarten and transition classes continued to use that property. In 1993 the school bought over 204 Nithsdale Road, money for which came from the sale of 328 Albert Drive.

A branch of Cochrane's on Albert Drive at the junction with Herriot Road. Andrew Cochrane became a tea trader in Glasgow in the early 1880s and by 1914 had built up a chain of approximately 100 grocery shops. These were bought over by Galbraiths, who in turn were bought over by Safeway, which was later taken over by Morrisons. Customer laundries were another type of business that became very popular in Glasgow from the 1880s, the first being in Jordanhill. At the end of Albert Road, where it met Darnley Street, was the Glasgow Steam Laundry and Carpetbeating Works. Founded by Thomas Donald in 1895, it remained in business for 60 years. Newly invented mechanical beaters provided the carpet-beating services.

Seen here at the corner of Albert Drive and Shields Road on 11 September 1958 is 'Cunarder' tram 1332. It came into service on 3 May 1950 and was scrapped on 7 September 1962. The large villa behind the tram was one of many villas erected in Pollokshields from 1851 onwards. Between 1888 and 1907 the most prolific builders of the villas were the architects James Marr and George Hamilton. Directly opposite this villa is 'The Knowe', built in 1856 and the earliest surviving Glasgow villa designed by Alexander 'Greek' Thomson. It was the first villa to be built away from St Andrew's Drive where the earliest had been erected in 1851. When 'The Knowe' was built, it was adjacent to Shields Farm. It was built for John Blair, who was a cap and hat manufacturer at 125 Trongate. By 1941 it was being used as a Salvation Army home for single mothers, and in the 1970s it was returned to residential use after an attempt to have it demolished. Modern flats have now been built within its grounds.

Knowe Terrace is only one of two in Pollokshields, the other being further along Shields Road at the brow of the hill. This terrace's design was heavily influenced by Greek Thomson's 'The Knowe', which is across the road (and for a time was known as 'Nilepark') but the identity of the architect remains a mystery. The chimney pots were modelled on the gate piers of 'The Knowe'. The valuation rolls for 1913/14 show the average value of a property in the terrace as £70 and feu duty ranged from £5/18/7d to £7/11/8d. The residents were mainly professionals, such as dentists, surgeons, merchants and engineers.

E. Murray & Co. was a printing company in Darnley Street, their premises being designed by Gordon, Son, Dobson and Sturrock in 1903/04. This photograph was taken in 1907. The building to the right is an A-listed building of national architectural interest as it has virtually complete Art Nouveau office interiors on the first floor. It was designed in 1902 by D.B. Dobson, a skilled Art Nouveau designer of Gordon and Dobson, for the art publishers, Millar and Lang. This firm also had an office in London. The building had sides of brick, unlike the rest of the buildings in Pollokshields which have stone all around. Millar and Lang produced many postcards in the early 1900s including those for the Festival of Empire Exhibition and Pageant of London at Crystal Palace in 1911. The company went into liquidation in 1982 and their Scottish postcard assets were acquired by Whiteholme (Publishers) Dundee, a company established by two of the former workers of the postcard publishers J.B. White & Co. of Dundee. The building is now owned by John McCormick & Co Ltd, printers, a firm established in 1890.

The view from Darnley Gardens would look directly onto the railway line belonging to the Caledonian Railway's Strathbungo and General Terminus Connecting Branch line. The nearest stations were Strathbungo and Pollokshields West. Strathbungo Station was opened on 1 December 1877 and was originally part of the Glasgow, Barrhead & Kilmarnock Joint Railway. It closed permanently to passengers on 28 May 1962. The line is still open as part of the Glasgow South Western line. Pollokshields West Station was part of the Cathcart District Railway which, in 1923, became part of the London, Midland and Scottish Railway. It is now part of the Cathcart Circle Line.

The earliest tenements in the burgh were at the west end of Maxwell Road and date from around the 1860s. Those in Leven Street, seen here, were probably built in the mid 1870s. The feu conditions for Nether Pollok did not allow shared or outside toilets and all flats also had baths. This was in complete contrast to standards in the city of Glasgow. Many of the occupants of the Pollokshields tenements were tenants on a lease, so the owners of the properties had a source of income. Rents varied from between £22 and £50 per annum.

It is difficult to believe that at the other end of Shields Road from this picture there were major railway lines at Shields Junction with three different railway stations: Pollokshields Station on the Glasgow & Paisley Joint line was at 312 Shields Road, Shields Road Station on the City of Glasgow Union line was at 326 Shields Road, and Shields Station on the Glasgow & South Western's Paisley Canal line was at 350 Shields Road. Built in the mid 1880s, they were combined as New Shields Road Station in April 1925. The Glasgow, Paisley & Ardrossan Canal, which later – after it was filled in – formed the route of the Glasgow & South Western's Paisley Canal railway line, ran parallel with the rail track. Between the canal and the Glasgow & Paisley Joint line were the Caledonian Railway's lines which diverged at Shields Bridge.

The church in the background of this 1951 view of Sheilds Road is St Albert's RC Church in Albert Drive. The tram in the foreground was on route 12. The Glasgow Standard cars were introduced in 1898 and remained in operation until 1961. In total, 1,005 were built to serve the city and surrounding areas. One of the difficulties with route 12 was its very sharp curves, and consequently modern trams were not seen on that line. In 1958 the route was replaced with a trolleybus service.

Taken at the corner of Shields Road and McCulloch Street, Deans at the corner is now a branch of Ladbrokes with Southside Housing Association next door. Advertised in the window at the left of the photograph is Allsopp's Pale Ale. Samuel Allsopp & Sons was one of the largest brewery companies operating in Burton upon Trent. Allsopp's began in the 1740s, when Benjamin Wilson, an innkeeper-brewer of Burton, brewed beer for his own premises and sold some to other innkeepers. In 1822 he copied the India Pale Ale of Hodgson, a London brewer, and by 1861 Allsopps was the second largest brewery after Bass. Allsopps fell into the hands of the receivers in 1911, but the company's capital was restructured and it continued trading. In 1935 Samuel Allsopp & Sons merged with Ind Coope Ltd to form Ind Coope and Allsopp Ltd. The Allsopp name was dropped in 1959 and in 1971 Ind Coope was incorporated into Allied Breweries.

Seen here at Nithsdale Cross, the corner of Albert Drive and Nithsdale Road, is Standard car 748 heading for the University of Glasgow. The tram began service in 1900 and was scrapped in 1955. Part of the route would take the tram along Mosspark Boulevard, the only evidence left of the tramlines there being the wide grassy area at the side of Bellahouston Park. The terminus at the university changed in 1959 when repairs were being made to the bridge in Gibson Street; after that, services were diverted to Park Road. Development of the area north of Nithsdale Road and bounded by Albert Drive began in 1851 and was complete by the mid 1870s.

The Coronation car on Route 3 is pictured here just outside Sherbrooke St Gilbert's Church of Scotland. On an elevated site at the corner of Sherbrooke Avenue and Nithsdale Road is a large sandstone mansion, now the Sherbrooke Castle Hotel. John Morrison, a contractor whose wealth accumulated quickly at the time of Glasgow's building boom, constructed the house himself. It dates from 1896 and was designed by Thomson and Sandilands. Morrison also built the Royal Princess's Theatre – now the Citizens'. His company was the chief contractor for such buildings as the City Chambers in George Square, the Clyde Trust Buildings in Robertson Street and Coats Memorial Church in Paisley. The company also built Craigmaddie Reservoir and tunnels as part of the fresh water system for Glasgow. During the Second World War the building was requisitioned by the Royal Navy and used as a radar training station.

The junction of Maxwell Drive and Nithsdale Road. Maxwell Drive has the earliest surviving houses in Pollokshields, apart from 'The Knowe' in Albert Drive. Villas in Pollokshields were traditionally known by name – such as 'Ferndean', 'Cliff House', 'Birkwood', 'Leven View', 'Encliffe' and 'Vermont' – before the widespread use of street numbers was introduced. The names often reflected the interests of the original owners. The Consulate of Pakistan now has its premises at 45 Maxwell Drive in one of the original villas. Nowadays Nithsdale Road has the M77 motorway running under it, just behind where the tram is in the photograph. The first electric Standard tram route in Pollokshields began in November 1898. The route entered Pollokshields from Eglinton Toll along Maxwell Road (now part of Maxwell Drive), turning left into Kenmure Street, right into Albert Drive and left into St Andrew's Drive to its terminus at the junction with Nithsdale Road at Nithsdale Cross.

Originally Sherbrooke United Free Church, the hall opened in 1894 and the church in 1900. Designed by W.F. McGibbon, its organ was installed in 1910 by Norman & Beard. The congregation of St Gilbert's Church in Sherbrooke Avenue amalgamated with Sherbrooke in 1942. St Gilbert's was dismantled and rebuilt as Burnside Church in 1951. In 1994 Sherbrooke St Gilbert's was gutted by fire, but since then has been rebuilt by architect James Cuthbertson. When the church was restored, new stained glass was commissioned from Susan Bradbury of the Kilmaurs Stained Glass Partnership.

Many of the tenements in Pollokshields are generously sized, with four to six room flats being the norm. H.E. Clifford designed these white sandstone blocks at 44–84 Terregles Avenue. This block features paired bay windows, overhanging eaves, prominent drainpipes and chimneystacks. These designs are commonly associated with the 'Glasgow Style'. The houses have four, five or six rooms and a kitchen, arranged with two flats on a landing, entered from a central stair. The customary bed recess in the kitchen was expanded to form a small servant's bedroom and all the kitchens have a large pantry. The lobbies were only lit by lighting borrowed from the other rooms.

Facing Terregles Avenue across the cutting of the Cathcart Circle are the tenements in Fotheringay Road, erected in 1902. These are built in red sandstone and are slightly more elaborate than the white sandstone ones. Also designed by H.E. Clifford, they too are large, with a maid's room and bathroom. In 1933 a bronze plaque was erected at a tenement on the road to commemorate the birthplace of James A. Mollinson (1905–59). In July/August 1931 Mollison set a record time of eight days, 19 hours for a flight from Australia to England, and in March 1932 a record for flying from England to South Africa in four days, 17 hours. In 1932 he became the first person to fly non-stop and solo across the North Atlantic in a westerly direction. During one of his commercial flights, he met Amy Johnson, to whom he proposed only eight hours after meeting her, and while still in the air. Johnson accepted; they married on July 1932, but divorced in 1938. Behind Fotheringay Road in Kirkcaldy Road are Edwardian tenements dating from 1907–09. On the south side of the road are Titwood Athletic Grounds, home to Clydesdale Cricket Club. Although founded in Kinning Park in 1848, the club moved to Pollokshields in 1875. The pavilion of the club was designed by H.E. Clifford.

When Titwood Bowling and Tennis Club opened in 1890, the club had two greens and a clubhouse designed by architects Messrs Clark and Bell. Sir John Maxwell gave his patronage to the club and served as Honorary President along with Provost John Murray, West Pollokshields, as Honorary Vice President. In 1898 the club opened a third green, giving it the unique status of being the only Scottish club with three full-sized greens. For many years, an annual match was held with Glasgow Corporation Bowling Club. Introduced in 1949, the club badge includes the personal crest and motto of Sir John Stirling Maxwell – 'I am ready'. In its first year, the tennis club had 211 members and another 55 held joint bowling and tennis membership. In Scotland in general, there was a large decline in tennis club membership, possibly due to the surge of interest in cycling, so in 1898 a decision was made to dissolve the tennis section and the courts were allowed to lie derelict until 1903. A new enthusiasm for tennis meant the club was resurrected and is still in existence today. The clubhouse and pavilion was completed in 1925 and opened by Lady Weir. In the 1990s lights on the courts were installed and the blaes courts were replaced with new all-weather surfaces which were opened on 27 April 1996.

Kingston Bowling Club at McCulloch Street and Kenmure Street, seen here, was founded in 1849 and moved to Pollokshields in 1872 after Sir John Stirling Maxwell provided the land exclusively for bowling. It closed in 2008. Pollokshields Bowling Club opened its doors in 1862, but also closed in 2008. It was situated at the corner of Maxwell Drive and St John's Road.

At the junction of Kenmure Street and Nithsdale Road is an area known as Kitchin's Corner, seen here in May 1928. Originally the pharmacy formed part of a shopping complex that consisted of four small shops, the entrance to which led into a passageway to the rear of the property. The alteration to the property took place in 1883 when the ground floor flats of the neighbouring property were being converted into shops. Their gardens were removed to create wider pavements. However, work to the complex was abandoned and the entrance was filled in with three vertical windows. Beside Kitchin's pharmacy, was William B. Paterson's grocery. In the 1930s there was a tobacconist, John Drysdale. The picture also shows a post office to the right of Paterson's.

The tobacconist at the left of this May 1928 view of Kenmure Street is advertising Muratti cigarettes. Bill Murattis was a Greek tobacco businessman in Constantinople in the nineteenth century who decided to move his company to London. For over 100 years 'Bill Murattis and Sons' manufactured many premium blends. The only Muratti cigarette still on the market is Muratti Ambassador, which is now one of the brands owned by Philip Morris International.